POEMS TO STIMULATE AND INSPIRE THE CURIOUS MINDS

PRANAB KUMAR DAS GUPTA

Jurisdiction: All disputes related to publication shall be subject to the jurisdiction of the Courts, Tribunals and Forums of Baleshwar, Odisha, India 756001 only.

Price: Rs 250

ISBN: 978-93-342-7913-9

Disclaimer: The information provided in this book is intended for general informational purposes only. The opinions expressed herein belong to the author and do not necessarily represent the official stance of any individual, agency, organization, employer, or company. Although the author and publisher have taken great care to ensure the accuracy and comprehensiveness of the information in this book, they do not accept responsibility for any errors, inaccuracies, omissions, or inconsistencies contained within. Any reliance on the information presented is entirely at your own risk. The author and publisher disclaim any liability for any loss or damage (including indirect or consequential loss) that may arise directly or indirectly from the use of, or reliance on, the content in this book. Mentions of specific commercial products, processes, or services using trade names, trademarks, manufacturers, or otherwise do not indicate endorsement, recommendation, or preference by the author or publisher. This book does not serve as a substitute for professional advice across legal, medical, financial, or any other fields. Readers are advised to seek appropriate professional assistance tailored to their individual circumstances.

CREATION OF THE COVER

The book cover is a visual meditation on the poet's creative consciousness, blending geometry and symbolism into a harmonious design.

Central Element: A stylized head diagram represents the poet's mind - structured yet boundless. Within it, staircases ascend like thoughts **(∞)** to thoughtless (0) in meditation, while embedded logic symbols reflect the interplay of reason and intuition.

Top Left (∞): The infinite, symbolizing the formless divine.

Top Right (Diya): A flame for wisdom, dispelling ignorance.

Bottom Left (Shatkona): Uniting consciousness and energy.

Bottom Right (0): Where beginnings end, and endings begin.

Foundation: The author's name, Pranab Kumar Das Gupta, anchors the design in earthly identity, while a thin horizontal line, mirroring the bridge between individual and universal.

Colour: Vibrant yellow, the hue of intellect and solar vitality - invokes inspiration.

Book Structure: The 108-page count honours the mala bead tradition, framing the poetic journey from spark (1) to surrender (0) to expression (8).

DEDICATION

To the timeless wisdom of the Bhagavad Gita and the divine guidance of Shree Krishna, whose teachings illuminate the path of self-discovery, challenge the mind, and awaken the soul. May this collection of poems embrace life's wonder and its profound truths. With deepest gratitude to all who seek meaning and beauty in the journey of existence.

TABLE OF CONTENT

PREFACE

Welcome to "Poems to Stimulate and Inspire the Curious Mind" a collection crafted to ignite your imagination, challenge your perspectives, and stir your soul. This book is not merely a compilation of verses; it is an invitation to embark on a journey of introspection, discovery, and wonder.

Each poem in this collection is a window into a unique thought, emotion, or idea, designed to resonate with the curious mind. To enhance your experience, every poem is accompanied by a sketch that visually captures its essence, offering a deeper connection to its theme. The themes themselves are thoughtfully presented, allowing you to explore the heart of each piece before diving into the verses. At the end of each poem, you will find a distilled essence a nugget of insight to provoke further thought and inspire deeper contemplation.

While the majority of the poems are self-explanatory, crafted to speak directly to your intuition and emotions, some delve into more complex ideas. For these, I have included brief explanations to guide your understanding and enrich your reflection.

This book is for the dreamers, the thinkers, and the seekers. It is for those who find beauty in questions and solace in exploration. Whether you are a seasoned lover of poetry or a curious newcomer, I hope these poems spark something within you a new idea, a forgotten emotion, or a fresh perspective.

Thank you for allowing me to share this journey with you. May these poems provoke your mind, inspire your spirit, and leave you with a sense of wonder long after you turn the final page.

Happy Reading!

Pranab Kumar Das Gupta

ACKNOWLEDGMENTS

I am profoundly grateful to all those who have played an indispensable role in bringing this book to fruition. Their unwavering support, guidance, and encouragement have been the cornerstone of this journey.

First and foremost, I extend my heartfelt gratitude to my beloved family and siblings for their constant encouragement and steadfast belief in my abilities. Their love and support have been my greatest source of strength.

I would like to express my deepest appreciation to my sisters Shikha, Maya, Prabha, Surekha, Alka, Radha, Poushali, Minakshi, Urmi, and Sumi for their invaluable contributions, particularly in shaping the cover of this book. Their creative insights and thoughtful suggestions have added a unique charm to its presentation.

I am immensely thankful to my esteemed superiors Dr. Samir V. Kamat, Dr. B.K. Das, Prof. Prateek Kishore, and Mr. S.K. Nayak for their professional support and understanding. Their encouragement and flexibility allowed me the time and space to dedicate myself to this literary endeavour.

My sincere thanks go to Danijeulu for his meticulous attention to detail, ensuring that this book looks impeccable. His dedication and precision have been instrumental in refining the final product.

I extend my deepest gratitude to the ever-evolving realm of technology, where artificial intelligence - like ChatGPT's whispered suggestions, DeepSeek's thoughtful insights, and Canva's visual harmony - has become an unexpected muse, bridging imagination and form. These tools, gently guided by human intention, have helped refine and shape the verses within this collection. My exploration of this synergy between machine and metaphor led me to publish two books on the subject, their tables of contents awaiting you at the journey's end.

Finally, with profound reverence, I bow to the divine forces that guide and inspire me Lord Krishna, Lord Shiva, Surya Dev, and Bajrangbali. I humbly seek their blessings and wisdom as I continue to walk the righteous path of dharma, striving to fulfil my purpose with integrity and devotion.

Pranab Kumar Das Gupta

ABOUT THE AUTHOR

Dr. Pranab Kumar Das Gupta is a professional with more than 36 years of experience in Computer Science and HR management. Known for his leadership skills, training abilities, and career guidance, he has made significant contributions in his field.

Dr. Das Gupta holds an M.Sc., M.Tech, and Ph.D. in Computer Science. He has also enhanced his skills through executive training programs at top institutions like IIT Kharagpur, IIM Ahmedabad, IIM Kolkata, and IIM Lucknow.

Beyond his technical expertise, Dr. Das Gupta is a dedicated teacher, mentor, and poet. He is also a successful author, having written 12 books related to Computer Science and Management. His ability to share valuable life lessons through his work has motivated him to pen this book.

1

THE POWER OF SILENCE

This touching story highlights the mindfulness, showing how inner calm can reveal what truly matters.

An old man sat with grief untold,
A watch was lost, its memory gold -
A gift from his wife, now gone above,
A token of her endless love.

Through garden paths he searched in vain,
His heart ached with a weight of pain.
Children played, their laughter bright,
He called for help to set things right.

"I'll gift you well," he pledged the crowd,
"Find my watch, and make me proud."
They scurried far, they tried, they pried,
But hope soon faded - none espied.

The old man sat, his head hung low,
No sign of his watch, no place to go.
But one small boy, with a quiet plea,
Asked for a chance to search carefully.

The boy sat still, calm and aware,
Hearing the whispers of the air.
A tick-tick hum, so faint, so slight,
Drew him like a star guides night.

Within moments, he returned,
The watch secured, its glint affirmed.
The old man wept, his heart at peace,
As sorrow's knots began release.

The boy had shown a lesson true:
What rush obscures, the still will view.
Let silence lead where noise has flown -
The deepest things are heard, not shown.

Breath held still, both in and out,
Mind released from fear and doubt.
Eyes fixed gently 'tween the brows,
Silence deep - the soul allows.

In power of silence, senses fall,
He walks within, beyond them all.
From Bhagavad Gita Shloka 5.27 and 28,
Meditation opens the inner gate.

ESSENCE

In silence, lost treasures are found.

2

A FATHER'S SILENT SORROW

This tender poem unveils a father's silent love, where pride meets pain. A moving tale of letting go, woven with cherished memories and unspoken sacrifices.

A daughter's marriage, a father's pain,
A heart-wrenching moment, a love in vain.
He bids farewell to his little girl dear,
And hides his emotions, and wipes away a tear.

He's expected to be strong, to show no fear,
To maintain a stoic demeanour, year by year.
But deep inside, his heart is breaking slow,
Into a million pieces, as his baby girl grows.

He walks her down the aisle, with steps so fine,
But every glance, a reminder, of a love divine.
He struggles to hold back tears, as he gives her away,
And feels the pain of letting go, with each passing day.

Mothers, sisters, and the bride, they cry and they sigh,
Their emotions flowing freely, as they bid goodbye.
But fathers, they're expected, to be strong and true,
To hide their emotions, and see their daughters
through.

He remembers the first time, he held her in his arms,
And felt an overwhelming sense, of pride and alarm.
First time she said "Papa", the first time she took a stride,
First time she went to school, and he felt his heart divide.

But now she's leaving, and he's left to grieve,
To mourn the loss, of his little girl, he used to receive.
He'll cherish the memories, of her childhood days,
And hold them close, in his heart's secret ways.

ESSENCE

A father's silent pain in daughter's farewell.

3

WHISPERS OF THE DIVINE

This reflective poem draws inspiration from the divine lives of Shri Ram and Shri Krishna, inviting readers to find strength and wisdom in their timeless stories.

In the quiet of our modern days,
We fret and falter, lost in the haze.
The weight of worries, the stress we bear,
Seems too immense, too hard to share.

Yet let us pause, and turn our gaze,
To lives divine, through time's long maze.
To Shri Ram, who walked in exile's night,
And Shri Krishna, born in peril's plight.

When crowns were dashed and hopes were torn,
Ram stood steadfast, though hearts were worn.
Fourteen years in forests deep,
He held his dharma, no time to weep.

And Krishna, born with death's dark chase,
A life of trials, yet a smiling face.
From poisoned milk to wars he'd face,
He taught the world divine grace.

The Gita's wisdom, a guiding light,
To act with duty, not fear the fight.
To trust the path, though shadows fall,
And rise above life's bitter call.

Oh, how we shrink from passing storms,
From fleeting aches, from fleeting forms.
Our comforts vast, our burdens small,
Yet still we crumble, still we sway.

Compare our lives to theirs, divine,
Who bore the weight of fate's design?
No luxury, no ease, no rest,
Yet in their hearts, they stood blessed.

So, when despair begins to creep,
And shadows darken, and spirits weep,
Remember Ram, remember Krishna's way,
And find the strength to face the day.

For stress and sorrow, though they sting,
Are but a part of life's vast ring.
And in their light, we learn to rise—
Not just to live, but sanctify.

So let us pause, and humbly pray,
To live as they did, come what may.
With faith, with duty, with hearts so true,
Our lives, like theirs, can shine anew.

EXPLAINATION

In times of stress and depression, turning to the lives of Shri Ram and Shri Krishna offers profound lessons on resilience, acceptance, and the philosophy of life. These divine figures, who are central to the teachings of the Bhagavad Gita, exemplify how to gracefully navigate life's challenges, no matter how severe they may seem.

Consider Shri Ram, the embodiment of dharma (righteousness). When the ceremony to coronate him as the King of Ayodhya was abruptly cancelled, and he was instead sent into exile for 14 long years, he accepted this sudden and drastic change without complaint. This moment, which could have led to immense stress and despair, was met by Shri Ram with calm acceptance and unwavering adherence to his duty. His reaction teaches us that life's unexpected hardships, no matter how painful, can be met with grace when we accept them as part of a larger divine plan.

Similarly, Shri Krishna's life was filled with trials and tribulations from the moment of his birth. Born into adversity, with repeated attempts on his life and countless struggles throughout his existence, Krishna's life could easily be considered one of the most challenging. Yet, despite these hardships, Krishna remained the eternal optimist, the divine strategist, and the compassionate guide. His teachings in the Bhagavad Gita encapsulate his philosophy on dealing with life's pressures: to perform one's duty without attachment to the results, to remain steadfast in the face of adversity, and to trust in the divine will.

These stories from the lives of Shri Ram and Shri Krishna illustrate that stress and depression are not new phenomena; they are intrinsic to the human experience. However, these divine figures show us how to confront these challenges with dignity and inner strength. The Bhagavad Gita, as a discourse delivered by Shri Krishna, serves as a guide for all of humanity, offering timeless wisdom on how to deal with life's inevitable struggles.

In essence, the lives of Shri Ram and Shri Krishna teach us that no matter how insurmountable our difficulties may seem, they are opportunities for growth and self-realization. The Bhagavad Gita offers a practical and spiritual approach to life, encouraging us to remain cantered, perform our duties, and maintain faith in the divine, even during the darkest of times. By internalizing these teachings, we can transform stress and depression into stepping stones toward a more profound and fulfilling existence.

4

TEJ PATTA'S (BAY LEAVES) STORY

This charming poem uses the metaphor of humble bay leaves in cooking to reflect on the often-overlooked efforts of those who work behind the scenes.

Tej Patta's a small bay leaf, so humble and fine,
It helps cook food, making it taste truly divine.
It's added first, to the hot oil in the pan,
And waits patiently, as the dish begins to take shape in hand.

It sees the veggies, spices, and herbs, one by one,
As the food transforms, minute by minute, till it's done.
The aroma rises, the flavors start to blend,
Tej Patta's hard work, is what makes the dish a true friend.

Then comes Dhaniya Patta, with a flourish and spin,
The coriander leaves, that add a fresh touch within.
It's sprinkled on top, like a celebrity's grand entrance,
And takes the credit, for the food's delightful essence.

But what about Tej Patta, who worked so hard and true?
It's thrown away, without a thank you, or a nod or two.
This happens often, in our daily lives, you see,
Where hard work goes unseen, and credit is denied, unfairly.

So, let's remember, to appreciate and see,
The efforts of others, who work hard with glee.
Let's value the Tej Pattas, who toil behind the scenes,
And recognize their worth, with a grateful heart and sincere themes.

ESSENCE

Unseen efforts matter, appreciate silent contributions.

5

THE GOLDEN YEARS OH, SO BRIGHT

This uplifting poem celebrates the golden years after 55, offering a vibrant guide to embracing self-care, personal growth, relationships, and joy.

After 55, it's time to play,
Use that savings, every single day!
Focus on self-care, don't be slow,
Eat, sleep, exercise, and watch your body glow!

Personal growth, it's time to explore,
Pursue those hobbies, and learn some more!
Stay informed, don't be in the dark,
Read, learn, and leave your mark!

Nurture relationships, don't let them fade,
Forgive, forget, and let love be displayed!
Surround yourself with cheerful folks,
Laugh, joke, and make those golden years rock!

Value independence, don't be a pest,
Respect your privacy, and take a rest!
Don't stress about the future or past,
Just live in the moment, and make it truly last!

Forgive and apologize, let go of the pain,
Enjoy life with your partner, and make love remain!
Respect the young, and their crazy views,
You were once young too, with wild dreams and shoes!

So, here's to the golden years, oh so bright,
Prioritize happiness, peace, and delight!
Make every day count, with joy and with cheer,
The golden years are here, so let's make them clear!

ESSENCE

Enjoy, grow, love, forgive—cherish golden years fully!

6

THE WEIGHT OF STRESS

This thought-provoking poem reveals a profound lesson about stress and the importance of letting go.

The room grew quiet; all eyes in place,
The presenter stood with a curious grace.
In his hand, a book so small,
Yet it seemed to hold the weight of all.

"Guess its weight," he asked with a grin,
A question that drew us all in.
"Two hundred grams?" someone did call,
"Five hundred, perhaps?" said another, enthralled.

He paused, then said, "The truth, I confess,
I don't know its weight—just take a guess.
But here's a twist to what you perceive,
Let me show you the truth I believe."

He raised the book, his arm held high,
"Hold it a minute, it's light as the sky.
But an hour will bring a throbbing ache,
And two—well, that's more than I'd take."

We leaned forward, caught in suspense,
His words were weaving a subtle sense.
"What's the trick?" we all wanted to know,
Why this book's weight seemed to grow.

He smiled and said, "It's all in the mind,
A lesson in stress you'll soon find.
Like this book, stress starts out light,
A fleeting shadow, a whisper of night.

But the longer you hold it, the more it grows,
Its weight will swell, as sorrow grows.
Cling for hours, it will break you down,
Days or weeks, and you'll surely drown.

So, when life's troubles come knocking near,
Don't clutch like stone, don't drown in fear.
Set them down, and you'll see the truth,
Relief lies in letting go, not in brute."

The room fell silent, his tale now told,
A lesson in stress, worth more than gold.
We left that day with a lighter heart,
For in letting go, true peace will start.

EXPLAINATION

During a stress management workshop, the presenter unexpectedly held up a copy of the Bhagavad Gita, leading the audience to brace themselves for yet another lecture on stress relief. Instead, he posed a simple question: "Can anyone guess the weight of this book?" This unexpected inquiry caught everyone off guard. The audience began to guess—"250 grams," one suggested; "maybe 500 grams," another ventured. After a short pause, the presenter smiled and admitted, "Honestly, I don't know the exact weight either."

He continued, "But here's something fascinating: If I hold this book for just a minute, it's easy. If I hold it for an hour, my arm begins to hurt. And if I try to bear it for two hours, the weight becomes unbearable. The longer I hold it, the heavier it feels."

The audience listened intently as he connected this metaphor to stress management. "This is how stress operates. A small amount of stress, akin to holding the book for a minute, can be manageable, even beneficial. However, the longer you cling to it, the heavier it becomes. Carry stress for days or weeks, and it can lead to severe issues like depression. So, when something troubles you, don't hold onto it for too long. Let it go for your own peace and happiness."

This poignant analogy provided the audience with a fresh perspective on stress management.

7

BEATS OF CONTRAST

This enchanting poem explores the contrasting powers of slow and fast, revealing how it nurtures the mind, body and soul.

Slow notes whisper, soft and low,
Melting tension's ebb and flow.
Fast beats spark like morning light,
Fuelling will to rise and fight.

Slow songs heal with deep embrace,
Pain dissolves without a trace.
Upbeat rhythms move our feet,
Setting life's quick pulse to beat.

Slow brings presence, keen and wise,
Seeing magic with new eyes.
Fast chords lift our hearts to play,
Chasing shadows far away.

Life flows like a song, fast or slow,
Through highs and lows, it comes and goes.
The key to peace is firm and true,
To stay the same in all you do.

The Gita speaks of wisdom deep,
A steady mind it longs to keep.
Through joy and pain, it stands so tall,
Unshaken by the rise and fall.

True freedom lies in work well done,
Not chasing prizes, lost or won.
With heart detached, yet hands that try,
You'll find the peace within the sky.

ESSENCE

Detachment and equanimity - twin wings of liberation.

8

A MARITAL DANCE

This witty poem explores the universal dynamics of marriage, where wives voice dissatisfaction and husbands stay unaware. With humour and charm, it offers light-hearted` solutions to navigate the ups and downs of marital life.

It's a fact, a phenomenon so fine,
Wives express dissatisfaction, a common sign.
"How did I end up with this guy?" they secretly sigh,
Feelings of neglect, forgetfulness, and uselessness in the eye.

Wives derive energy from expressing their plight,
Husbands, oblivious, wearing oblivious armour so tight.
But when criticisms cease, and the dynamic shifts,
Husbands feel uneasy, with a puzzled, worried lift.

A strategy to address this issue, so simple, yet so grand,
Employ logic, empathy, and humour, hand in hand.
Acknowledge the universality of this marital test,
Your wife feelings are not unique, but truly blessed.

Perhaps ninety-nine partners play this game,
A remarkable statistic, a truth to proclaim.
The one who doesn't, a sign of a bigger storm,
A calm before the cyclone, a silence that's not norm.

So, let's be realistic, and put things in perspective too,
If you had married another, the dynamics would still shine through.
It's not about me, or you, or our relationship so fine,
It's about the universal challenges, that come with marriage's divine.

So, let's focus on the beauty, of our imperfections so rare,
And the love that we share, with all its ups and downs, with care.
And if all else fails, and we can't agree,
Let's order some pizza, and laugh, wild and free!

ESSENCE

Marriage thrives on humour, empathy, and minor fight.

9

SUSHUMNA'S AWAKENING

This enlightening poem unveils the ancient wisdom of breath observation, offering profound insights into physical and mental well-being.

In today's fast-paced world we live,
A simple breathing exercise can help us give,
Insight into our physical fitness and brain,
Try it out and discover the benefits you'll gain.

Find a quiet spot, sit comfortably too,
Inhale deeply, exhale, and observe anew,
The nostril from which your breath does flow,
Take note of time and side, let your awareness grow.

Set an alarm for an hour, then observe once more,
You'll likely find the breath flows from the opposite shore,
Ida and Pingala, subtle channels align,
Associated with brain hemispheres, a balance divine.

Ida Nadi's breath from the left nostril flows free,
Activating the right brain hemisphere, creativity,
Emotions, intuition, and artistry shine bright,
A world of imagination, where innovation takes flight.

Pingla Nadi's breath from the right nostril does stride,
Activating the left-brain hemisphere, logic inside,
A laser of logic where insight takes hold,
Analysis, reasoning, and problem-solving skills unfold.

By observing your breath, you'll gain a deeper understanding true,
Of your physical and mental state, a new found awareness shines through.
If you're lucky, you may observe breath coming out from both nostrils,
Marking the activation of Sushumna Nadi, a wondrous sight to behold.

In yogic sciences, a secret's shared,
A state of balance, beyond compare.
Sushumna Nadi, a mystical flow,
Activates within, as breaths come and go.

With Ida and Pingla, a dance so fine,
Sushumna awakens, a balance divine.
Fifty minutes pass, and the state unfolds,
A window of clarity, young and old.

Early morning hours, a special time,
4:00 to 6:00, the activation's prime.
A catalyst for learning, a spark so bright,
Memorization and meditation, in plain sight.

Sixty minutes reduced to ten, a feat so grand,
Meditative states, achieved with an open hand.
Emotional and logical balance, a harmony so rare,
Critical decisions, made with clarity and care.

Daily practice becomes your master key,
Unlocking Sushumna's flow so free.
Early morning hours, a time to cultivate,
The benefits of Sushumna, a gift to participate.

Enhanced cognitive function, emotional balance too,
Decision-making acuity, a gift shining through.
Sushumna Nadi, a mystical flow so fine,
A secret to balance, a treasure divine.

EXPLANATION

In today's fast-paced world, maintaining physical and mental well-being is crucial. This simple breathing exercise can help you gauge your physical fitness and gain insight into your brain activity. Try it out and discover the benefits for yourself!

Step 1: Observe Your Breath

Find a quiet and comfortable place to sit. Inhale deeply and naturally. As you exhale, gently observe the nostril from which the breath is coming out. Take note of the time and the nostril side (left or right).

Step 2: Set an Alarm

Set an alarm for 1 hour. This will allow you to observe any changes in your breathing pattern.

Step 3: Observe the Change

When the alarm rings, exhale again and observe the nostril from which the breath is coming out. You will likely notice that the air is now coming out from the opposite nostril. For example, if the air was coming out from the left nostril initially, it will now be coming out from the right nostril, and vice versa.

Understanding the Results

This simple exercise reveals your physical fitness and provides insight into your brain activity. The two nostrils are associated with different nadis (energy channels) in the body:

- Ida Nadi (Left Nostril): When the air is coming out from the left nostril, your right brain hemisphere is active, which deals with emotional aspects, intuition, and creativity.

- Pingla Nadi (Right Nostril): When the air is coming out from the right nostril, your left brain hemisphere is active, which is responsible for physical aspects, logic, and analytical thinking.

By observing the change in your breathing pattern, you can gain a better understanding of your physical and mental state.

If you're lucky, you may observe breath coming out from both nostrils, marking the activation of Sushumna Nadi.

In yogic sciences, Sushumna Nadi activation is a highly sought-after state, renowned for its profound impact on cognitive function, emotional balance, and decision-making prowess. Typically achieved after 50 minutes of

Ida or Pingla Nadi dominance, this elusive state can last up to 10 minutes.

Research suggests that early morning hours, specifically between 4:00 a.m. and 6:00 a.m., offer a unique window for prolonged Sushumna Nadi activation. Sushumna Nadi activation serves as a catalyst, amplifying cognitive function and facilitating accelerated learning. Tasks like memorizing content, typically requiring 60 minutes, can be accomplished in just 10 minutes when Sushumna Nadi is active. Similarly, meditative states normally taking 40 minutes can be achieved in 10 minutes during activation. During Sushumna Nadi activation, individuals experience a unique state of emotional and logical balance, enabling them to make critical decisions free from bias, with heightened clarity and discernment.

Consistent practice and meditation can increase the duration of Sushumna Nadi activation, particularly during early morning hours. By cultivating this state, individuals can unlock numerous benefits, including enhanced cognitive function, emotional balance, and decision-making acuity.

10

ENJOY RETIREMENT

This soothing poem gently reminds us to embrace life's joys, let go of worries, and reconnect with ourselves and the divine, offering a heartfelt guide to living with peace, love, and grace.

Sleep more, worry less, it's time to unwind
Your children are settled, leave worries behind
Enjoy life's journey, explore and play
Rediscover hobbies that brighten up your day

Now that the kids are busy with their own screens,
You can finally eat those hidden ice creams!
No more sharing snacks or whispering "shhh...",
Your midnight fridge raids are now guilt-free—ahh!

Take time for self-reflection, look within your soul
Explore your passions, and make your heart whole
Devote time for God, in prayer or in thought
Connect with the universe, and let love be brought

Remember when you vowed "I'll sleep when I'm dead"?
Turns out zombies need naps—just like Mom said!
So fluff that pillow, steal one more snooze,
Responsibilities can wait for tomorrow's news.

Let go of stress, and let joy take its place
Smile, laugh, and live, with a heart full of grace
So sleep more, worry less, and enjoy life's ride
With love, laughter, and joy, deep inside.

Living long is not the way,
If peace and love are kept at bay.
A kind and purposeful life is best,
Bringing joy and gentle rest.

We turn from harm, with compassion show,
Helping hearts to bloom and grow.
To live each day with mindful grace,
Is to walk life's path in a sacred space.

In whispered chant, we seek the light—
Mahamrityunjay guides the soul's flight:
Om Tryambakam..., we softly say,
To heal, to bless, to clear our way.

ESSENCE

Relax, enjoy, reflect, embrace joy and peace.

11

UNLEASH YOUR MENTAL POTENTIAL

This poem shares a memory transformation through the power of Sanskrit and the Bhagavad Gita, offering how ancient wisdom can awaken the mind.

Back in school, oh what a plight,
Memorizing facts? A terrible fight!
History, geography—what a bore,
Dates and capitals? I'd rather snore!

Why rack my brain, why even try,
When Google's here with a single "Hi"?
A chocolate teapot—that was me,
Useless at facts, as you can see.

Names and numbers? Lost them all,
My memory skills were truly small!
Yet here I stand, quite amazed,
At fifty-eight, my brain's been raised!

Bhagavad Gita, verse by verse,
No more memory-wrecking curse!
Shlokas stuck where facts once fled,
Maybe Sanskrit rewired my head?

So, if I can do it, trust me, friend,
Your memory woes can also end!
So, chant a verse, give it a try,
Your brain will thank you, by and by!

Sanskritization, a path so bright,
An ancient tongue, a source of light.
With every word and verse we say,
Our minds grow sharper day by day.

It weaves a rhythm, rich and deep,
Awakens thoughts from slumbered sleep.
Memory blooms, so strong, so free,
Unfolding vast capacity.

With every sound, the mind takes flight,
A beacon glowing clear and bright.
Oh Sanskrit, gift of legacy,
A timeless key to sharp memory.

Unlock the power deep inside,
Let Sanskrit's wisdom be your guide.
With every shloka, pure and true,
A sharper mind awakens in you.

The Gita speaks in words so bright,
Dispelling darkness, bringing light.
Its chants will lift your soul so high,
Like soaring birds in endless sky.

No need to fear, don't turn away,
Just take the first small step today.
Pronounce, recite, and feel the sound,
A world of wisdom all around.

Your thoughts grow clear, your heart stands tall,
A balanced mind, the greatest call.
Memory sharp, intelligence bright,
Guided always by truth and light.

So why delay? The path is clear,
A journey grand is waiting near.
With Sanskrit's touch and Gita's grace,
Unlock your full potential's space.

Chant the shlokas, feel the change,
Watch your memory rearrange.
Sanskrit's power, Gita's light,
Make your mind both sharp and bright

ESSENCE

Sanskrit rewires, Gita inspires, memory fires.

12

KARMA AND REBIRTH

This intriguing poem journeys from the profound mysteries of Rebirth and Karma, inviting readers to reflect on fate, actions, and the cycles of existence.

A hypothesis, a simple start,
An idea accepted, plays its part.
In science and math, it lights the way,
Guiding our thoughts, day by day.

But life's complexities, vast and wide,
Need deeper truths to help us decide.
Two ancient ideas, Rebirth and Karma,
Explain the world, its joy and its drama.

Rebirth suggests a cycle we tread,
Lives lived again, where souls are led.
Past memories surface, behaviors unfold,
Stories of lives that were once told.

Karma says actions, good or bad,
Shape our future, joyful or sad.
A student who works hard reaps the reward,
While suffering may come from a past life's discord.

A corrupt soul may thrive, it seems,
From good deeds sown in past-life dreams.
Yet twins, though raised the same, may differ,
One thrives in health, the other grows stiffer.

Rebirth explains: two souls, two pasts,
Unique journeys, their fates are cast.
Karma adds weight, with deeds of old,
Shaping their stories, brave or bold.

Through Rebirth and Karma, we find our way,
To understand life, come what may.
Past actions shape the here and now,
A moral compass, a spiritual vow.

EXPLANATION

A hypothesis is an assumption that is accepted as true for the sake of argument or further study. The first hypothesis, Rebirth, suggests that individuals go through a cycle of births and deaths. There are numerous stories and cases where people remember past lives. The second hypothesis, Karma, states that our actions—whether good or bad—have consequences, either in this life or in future ones. We often observe the effects of Karma in everyday life. For example, a hardworking student is likely to achieve good grades and secure a good job. On the other hand, we sometimes see good people who suffer greatly. This could be because, in a past life, they committed a very bad act and were never punished, perhaps because they died before facing the consequences. According to Karma, these unresolved actions do not disappear; they carry over into future lives, causing the suffering we witness now.

Similarly, when we see a corrupt person living a comfortable life, it might be due to good Karma from past lives. The comforts they enjoy now could be rewards for good deeds in a previous life.

Why do we see significant differences between twins, even when they have the same parents, environment, and schooling? How can one twin be healthy while the other is not, despite growing up under the same conditions? These differences can be explained by Rebirth and Karma. The healthy twin might be reaping the benefits of good actions in a past life, while the other could be dealing with the consequences of bad actions from a past life.

By accepting the ideas of Rebirth and Karma, we can find logical explanations for the varied experiences in our lives and those of others.

13

FRESH VEGGIES FROM THE MARKET!

This funny poem follows a husband's market mishap as he messes up his wife's veggie list. His wife's playful scolding turns his blunder into a hilarious lesson.

Oh, husband dear, I have a list for you,
To fetch from the market, fresh and new.
Eight veggies, with weights defined,
Bring them home, and ease my mind!

Broccoli, 250 grams, a healthy delight,
Spinach, 400 grams, packed with iron's might.
Carrots, 1.2 kilos, and one kilo onions, crisp and sweet,
Ladies finger, 500 grams, a crunchy treat!

Tomatoes, 800 grams, and potatoes, 1.5, divine,
Pumpkin, 1.8 kilos - make sure it's fine!
Remember the weights, and don't you dare,
Bring home the wrong ones - handle with care!

Off he went, with a confident stride,
But forgot the list, and his memory died.
He came home grinning, with bags in hand,
But his wife's raised eyebrow made him take a stand.

"What's this?" she said, with a teasing glare,
"You brought 200g instead of twelve hundred! Why are they there?
And 500 grams of onions, instead of a kilo?
Where's the spinach and broccoli, though?"

He scratched his head, with a sheepish grin,
"I thought I'd improvise - and still win!
And look, I brought some extras, just for fun -
Bitter gourd and ridge gourd! Aren't I the one?"

She shook her head, with a playful smirk,
"Bitter gourd and ridge gourd? Oh, you do shirk!
These weren't on the list - what a surprise,
Next time, my love, you'll need to be wise!"

He checked the list again, his mistakes now clear,
250 grams of broccoli, not bitter gourd oh dear!
And remember 400 grams of spinach - what a shame,
He vowed to do better, and avoid the veggie blame.

So, husbands, take heed, and shop with care,
Check the list twice, and the weights - beware!
For a wife's veggie wrath is no small thing,
Get it right, or face her veggie-sling!

ESSENCE

Husband shops, memory flops, wife's fury pops.

14

THE MOUNTAIN OF GOLD

This captivating poem unfolds a timeless lesson on true generosity, contrasting two warriors' acts of giving and revealing the selfless spirit that defines the purest form of charity.

In a village where the rivers flow,
Two warriors walked, their steps slow.
Krishna spoke, his voice so wise,
"Who gives the most, beneath these skies?"

Arjuna paused, his pride held high,
"Who could it be?" he dared reply.
"Karna," said Krishna, calm and clear,
"The greatest giver, far and near."

Arjuna's heart, with doubt, did churn,
For Karna's worth he'd yet to learn.
Then Krishna waved, and lo, appeared,
A golden mountain, grand and revered.

"Take this gold, and prove your grace,
Give to the villages, your love embrace."
Arjuna toiled from dawn to night,
Distributing gold till the fading light.

Through villages wide, he spread his cheer,
Ensuring none were left in fear.
His arms grew tired, his spirit worn,
Yet pride within him still was born.

As shadows stretched, a figure came,
Karna approached; his heart aflame.
Krishna spoke, "This gold is yours,
Give as you will, open the doors."

Karna smiled, his voice so clear,
"Villagers, come, have no fear.
This mountain of gold is yours to share,
Take what you need, it's yours to bear."

No pause, no praise, no second thought,
He gave it all, as if it were *not*.
The villagers gasped, their eyes wide,
As Karna walked, with quiet pride.

Arjuna stood, his heart now still,
A lesson learned, a humbled will.
Krishna whispered, "Do you see?
True giving's done selflessly."

No need for fame, no need for show,
Just pure intent, a heart aglow.
For in the act of silent grace,
Lies the truest donor's place.

So let us learn from Karna's way,
To give without a need to sway.
For generosity's purest light,
Shines brightest when it's out of sight.

ESSENCE

Selfless generosity outshines.

15

SAGUN SAKAR & NIRGUN NIRAKAR

This thought-provoking poem beautifully explores three profound states of existence through vivid metaphors, inviting readers to reflect on the visible, the unseen, and the infinite.

In the glow of a bulb, Sagun Sakar shines,
A shape so clear, its light defines.
The glass, the filament, a form we see,
Yet within it dances energy, wild and free.

Sagun Nirakar whispers, a mystery untold,
Electricity's essence, neither young nor old.
No shape, no face, yet its power we feel,
In the hum of machines, its presence is real.

It cools the air in the refrigerator's embrace,
And warms the room when the heater takes place.
A force unseen, yet shaping our plight,
Invisible, yet turning dark into light.

Then comes Nirgun Nirakar, vast and unbound,
A lightning strike, where no form is found.
No vessel to hold it, no hand to tame,
A spark of the infinite, no two the same.

It cracks the sky, a fleeting display,
A glimpse of the cosmos, then fades away.
Brief as dawn's first golden ray,
Swift as thought that won't obey.

Sagun Sakar glows in light so bright,
Sagun Nirakar flows, a hidden might.
Nirgun Nirakar, vast and free,
A fleeting spark of eternity.

EXPLAINATION

The concepts of Sagun Sakar, Sagun Nirakar, and Nirgun Nirakar can be challenging to comprehend. However, Shankaracharya of Puri has provided elucidating explanations of these concepts through various video lectures, supplemented with numerous examples.

To illustrate, consider the analogy of a light bulb. In this context, Sagun Sakar refers to the tangible aspects of the bulb, where the physical shape of the bulb (Sakar) and the light it emits (Sagun) are both perceivable.

In contrast, Sagun Nirakar can be exemplified by electricity. While the source of electricity remains unknown (Nirakar), its effects are manifest when harnessed to power devices like air conditioners or heaters. Here, electricity embodies Nirgun (formless), and the resultant cooling or heating effects represent Sagun (manifested qualities).

Lastly, Nirgun Nirakar denotes an infinite, formless energy. A striking example of this concept is lightning, which lacks a discernible shape and cannot be contained. This phenomenon epitomizes the essence of Nirgun Nirakar.

16

SHE AND HE:

A PERFECT HARMONY

This powerful poem envisions highlight the irreplaceable role of women, celebrating their strength and resilience.

Imagine a world where men fade away,
Life would still bloom, women would stay.
Pregnant mothers, with dreams burning bright,
Would birth sons and daughters under the skies.

Through women alone, life's thread would weave,
A future sustained, if men were to leave.
But picture a world where women are gone,
The human race would soon come undone.

No life to nurture, no child to bear,
Silence would choke the empty air.
A stark reminder, so clear, so true,
Women's role is vital in all that we do.

A woman's heart is soft and true,
Like gold that shines in every hue.
She's gentle, pure, and full of grace,
With love and warmth in her embrace.

A man is like the brass so strong,
Built to guard and help along.
Though not as rare, his worth is clear,
A steady hand, a shield from fear.

Gold needs care and careful touch,
Its value lies in feeling much.
Brass stands firm through storm and strife,
A partner strong in work and life.

But trouble starts when roles are blurred,
When natural ways go unheard.
For gold to shine, it must stay bright,
And brass must guard with all its might.

When both are true to who they are,
Together they can reach so far.
In love and strength, hand in hand,
They build a life both bold and grand.

ESSENCE

Without women, silence reigns; with them, life thrives.

17

ECHOES OF THE INFINITE

This thought-provoking poem contrasts the vastness of the universe with human pride, offering a witty reflection on our place in the grand cosmic expanse.

In endless space, so vast, so wide,
A universe no words can describe.
Galaxies shine in cosmic streams,
Each with stars and distant dreams.

Among them spins a tiny sphere,
Earth, where humans first appear.
In Asia's lands, so rich, so bright,
India glows with vibrant light.

West Bengal stands with culture deep,
While Kolkata's streets forever speak.
Thousands of homes, where families stay,
With love and dreams to light the way.

Yet, within this grand expanse,
A funny truth, a strange romance—
Tiny beings, proud and strong,
Thinking they control it all along.

Each believes they know the best,
Wiser, greater than the rest.
With egos vast, like stars so high,
As if they own the endless sky.

Oh, what humour, what a sight,
Mere dust pretending to hold might.
Fighting, shouting, making a scene,
As if the universe cares what they mean.

So go ahead, inflate your pride,
Shout your greatness, swollen with pride.
The stars just sigh, the planets spin,
And no one knows you've ever been.

ESSENCE

Universe laughs at our fleeting pride.

18

soul.exe

INSTALLING CREATIVITY IN A MACHINE

AI is a powerful tool, but human creativity, discipline, and spiritual wisdom must guide it for true success.

AI is rising, swift and bright,
A tool of power, sharp with might.
It helps us work, it saves us time,
Yet wisdom makes its purpose shine.

Let it serve but not command,
Guide it with a steady hand.
For mindless trust in AI's thought
May leave our gifts to come to naught.

Creativity must lead the way,
With vision clear, it lights our day.
No program, no machine can find
The boundless dreams within our mind.

But skill alone is not enough,
Success requires a spirit tough.
With discipline, we build our way,
With strategy, we shape the day.

In work and life, with balance true,
Strong purpose drives all that we do.
With clear aims and steps designed,
We forge ahead with strength of mind.

Yet deeper still, we must explore,
The soul's own wisdom at its core.
For faith and purpose light the way,
And keep our hearts from going astray.

Spiritual depth and guiding grace
Help us move at the right pace.
For wealth and power mean so small
If we lose our soul through it all.

EXPLANATION

If you are not leveraging Artificial Intelligence (AI) in your work or daily life, you risk falling behind in an increasingly competitive world. AI is an invaluable tool—an efficient assistant, a dedicated personal secretary, and a powerful productivity enhancer. However, it must always remain a servant, not a master.

While AI adoption is rapidly expanding, simply using it without integrating creativity, strategic thinking, and spiritual awareness will not be enough. In the near future, when AI becomes a common tool for all, those who fail to combine it with innovation, strong personal and professional management skills, and a deeper sense of purpose will struggle to stay relevant.

Spirituality provides inner stability, ethical grounding, and clarity of purpose, while effective personal and professional management ensures disciplined execution and growth. Those who integrate these elements, accelerating their output through AI while maintaining their unique value, will be highly sought after by industries.

To thrive in the AI-driven era, professionals must balance technology with creativity, personal and professional management capabilities, and spirituality. AI enhances productivity, but true success comes from critical thinking, adaptability, and ethical decision-making. Spirituality fosters self-awareness and purpose, guiding individuals to use AI responsibly.

19

TEARS OF THE SOUL

Tears - whether born of joy or sorrow - are a natural, healing expression of our deepest emotions and proof of our capacity for love and connection.

Tears may fall in joy or feeling,

Like the dew, a gentle healing.

Laughter spills, and eyes will gleam,

Flowing softly like a stream.

Stories told with hearts laid bare,

Reveal depths we're moved to share.

Memories, both old and new,

Find their truth in teardrops too.

In our sorrow, in delight,

Tears can make our burdens light.

Not a weakness - rather strong,

Proof that love has lived so long.

Through joy and sorrow, tears will flow,

A sign of love that we all know.

They show we're real, both strong and true,

Engaged, empathetic, and authentic too.

Let them fall in times of cheer,

Let them shine when feeling's near.

For in every drop that flows,

Lies the love our soul bestows.

ESSENCE

Emotions flow authentically.

20

THE HEAVY WAIT

This poem explores the modern anxiety of seeking validation through digital connections, where silence often feels like rejection, leaving us questioning our worth.

In a world so loud, yet silent too,
We seek a voice, a sign, a view.
A like, a share, a message read,
But silence lingers here instead.

The heart beats fast, the mind in doubt,
"Do they care? Do I stand out?"
The waiting game, the endless stream,
A pixelated, fractured dream.

We tie our worth to words and praise,
To fleeting moments, to passing gaze.
A post, a thought, a heartfelt call,
Met with silence—do we fall?

The stress, the doubt, the lonely night,
The hollow glow of artificial light.
A heart once full, now feels so small,
Trapped by hopes that rise and fall.

But in the quiet, a whisper grows,

A truth that ancient wisdom knows.

From the *Gita*, these words take flight:

कर्मण्येवाधिकारस्ते मा फलेषु कदाचन।

(You have the right to act, but not to the fruits of action.)

मा कर्मफलहेतुर्भूर्मा ते सङ्गोऽस्त्वकर्मणि।

(Do not let results drive you, nor avoid your duty.)

Do your duty, let go of gain,

Do not let loss bring you pain.

Your right is action, pure and true,

Not in what comes back to you.

Act with love, but let it flow,

Expecting nothing in return to show.

For every heart fights battles unseen,

Not all neglect is meant to demean.

Find joy in sharing, in giving light,
Not in echoes, nor in sight.
Your worth is yours, it stands so tall,
Not built by likes, nor made to fall.

Let silence come, let voices fade,
Let actions shine, let fears evade.
No praise, no blame, can shake your soul,
When you embrace a higher goal.

A heart unchained, a mind set free,
A spirit soaring endlessly.
Not bound by screens, nor words unsaid,
But full of life, by love instead.

For silence is not void or lack—
It's where the soul finds its way back.
A space to breathe, to heal, to grow,
A light within, a steady glow.

If one verse alone can heal the mind,
Imagine the wisdom you will find.
A book of truth, so vast, so deep,
With lessons strong, for souls to keep.

It lights the way through joy and strife,
A guide to live a balanced life.
So read the *Gita*, embrace its grace,
And walk this world with strength and peace.

ESSENCE

Detach. Act. Shine.

21

WISDOM FOR A WORLD OF DIGITAL DECEIT

Scams exploit human weakness, but ancient wisdom teaches protection through self-awareness.

In this world of screens so bright,
Scammers lurk both day and night.
They prey on hopes, they twist the truth,
They steal from elders, trick the youth.

With words so sweet and dreams so grand,
They offer wealth with sleight of hand.
A love so pure, a fortune near,
They play on trust, they feed on fear.

Phishing emails, fake romance,
Crypto schemes that promise chance.
"Click this link, just share your code,"
They leave you stranded, crushed, erode.

Deepfake videos, voices cloned,
A loved one's plea, but it's a con.
"Send me money, I'm in distress,"
A heartless ploy, a cruel mess.

Greed and lust, the traps they weave,
Make hearts too quick to trust, believe.
A promised gain, a whispered lie,
Can leave one broke with tears to dry.

But wisdom old, from times long past,
Can guide us safe and make us last.
The Gita speaks of dangers three -

Greed, lust, and wrath - so let them be.

त्रिविधं नरकस्येदं द्वारं नाशनमात्मनः।
कामः क्रोधस्तथा लोभस्तस्मादेतत्त्रयं त्यजेत्॥
"Three gates to ruin trap mankind -"
"Lust, greed, and wrath that cloud the mind."
"Abandon these," Lord Krishna speaks,
"Or fall to sorrow that one reaps."

These words, though ancient, still hold true,
A guiding light for me and you.
For scams today, though dressed in new,
Exploit the same faults we must subdue.

With patience, thought, and steps so wise,
We break the web of fraud and lies.
So, doubt the deals too good to see,
And love that comes too easily.

Pause and think before you act,
Question motives, check the facts.
A moment's care can save the day,
And keep deceit's traps at bay.

For in the Gita, truth remains,
A guide through joys and through our pains.
Its wisdom lights the path we tread,
Protecting heart, and soul, and head.

If one small verse can light the way,
The Gita holds much more to say.
Though times may change, our hearts still yearn,
In ancient wisdom, truth returns.

So let us learn, reflect, and grow,
The Gita's light will help us know—
Not just in wealth, but thought and deed,
A life of wisdom, free from greed.
Take heart, dear friend, and tread with care,
For scammers thrive where minds aren't aware.
With Gita's light and truth's bright flame,
We guard our souls and break their game.

Through every age, through every test,
The Gita's truths remain our quest.
In patience, thought, and self-control,
We find the strength to make us whole.

ESSENCE

Shun greed and lust to evade scams.

22

RAISING SUCCESSFUL (AND HAPPY) CHILDREN

Reconnect through love, not screens; guide with wisdom, not pressure - the Gita's light restores childhood's joy and parenting's purpose.

In childhood's light, we once did play,
But now, we drive our kids each day -
To chase the dreams we left behind,
With marks and ranks that bind the mind.

We scroll through reels, we chat, we roam,
Yet claim we have no time at home.
Too tired to teach, we shift the blame,
Then gift them screens and feed the game.

No longer do they run and race,
Or feel the sun upon their face.
We called it smart, this digital art,
But drifted from the truest heart.

And as they grow, a gap appears,
With secrets, silence, doubts, and fears.
They think they're grown, they turn away,
And lose their path from light to grey.

Yet all is not beyond repair,

If we but love, and choose to care.

To teach, to guide with steady hand,

Not from control, but to understand.

If we are learned, let us start -

To share with them our thoughts, our quiet art.

Till Class 10, even Class 12's near,

Be present, be kind, and keep them near.

And children too, must see the thread,

Of love behind the words we've said.

For every parent's deepest pride,

Is seeing their child walk ahead with grace, not just in stride.

As the Gita's ancient voice implores -

Detach from fruit, let duty rise.

With trust, not fear, we shape the soul,

For life, not marks, should be the goal.

Let calmness bloom through every fall,
Let self-aware hearts hear the call.
With balance as our daily song,
Together, we grow wise and strong.

So walk with me, my child, my guide,
Through joy and pain, we stand, allied.
Not just in knowledge, but in grace,
With love and faith, we find our place.

The home becomes a sacred space,
Where wisdom walks with softest pace.
And in that light, both young and old,
Shall write their stories - brave and bold.

ESSENCE

Love guides, screens divide.

23

FROM PETALS TO PRICKLES

From 'Plant Marigold' Texts To 'Objection, Your Honour!'

In Southern Heights where cash flows free
A poll sparked rage Which flower shall it be
Petunias bright or marigolds bold
1042 messages chaos untold

The Admin quit their fate was sealed
Three resignations gardener revealed
I hope your lawns all turn to dust
His witness stand Pure spite and rust

Mrs Kapoor with fury untamed
Declared petunia lovers all insane
Ran to the cops samosas in hand
Book them for crimes against marigold land

FIR filed oh what a sight
They called them cheap its hate its spite
IPC 295A for floral slurs
Plus 4GB proof of text massacres

The Session Court sighed You are all a mess
While lawyers fought with soil duress
Petunias kill Marigolds depress
Judge ruled Plant sunflowers Swiss

High Court appeal more drama ensued
TED Talks on flowers Mood
CCTV showed Sharma's midnight theft
Judge groaned Just ROSE and leave me bereft

Then Supreme Court the final bout
Where AI proved Petunia cartels about
An intern dared whisper What of grass
Ejected fast justice moves fast

The verdict dropped like a spiky decree
CACTUS for all let silence be
No water no fights just sharp retorts
And stab the fools who clog the courts

Now WhatsApps renamed Cactus Hate

Mrs Kapoor lurks by the waste gate

The gardeners rich the lawns are dead

And cacti wear Court Order threads

Moral When bored elites with cash to burn

Make flowers a crime just sit and learn

The laws not blind its hungry see

Pro Tip Bring samosas And plant a tree

Legal Limerick A Disclaimer in Verse

Before the floral feud unfurls

Take heed dear reader truths in swirls

No plants were tried no fines were paid

All nonsense here is purely made

But if your group chat starts to fight

Just blame the cacti And goodnight

ESSENCE

Self-watering ego trees.

24

THE INVISIBLE WALL

An invisible wall divides us in conflict, but through listening, empathy, and collaboration, we can tear it down and rebuild with understanding.

Theres a wall we cannot see
It stands between both you and me
In every fight in every call
We hit this cold invisible wall

We talk and shout we try to explain
But words bounce back like echoes in a hollow hall
No one listens no one hears
Just growing silence growing fears

Let me tell you what we do
When conflict comes and breaks us in two
There are five paths we often take
Some bring peace some just heartache

Avoidance is the first we try
We close our eyes and pass it by
We hope the storm will fade away
But sometimes problems choose to stay
At home it may give kids the chance
To learn through their own little dance
But in the office quiet can burn
And soon the same old fights return

Then comes Competing loud and proud
Each voice above the other loud
In battles like exams or games
It's fair to fight and chase our aims

But when we try to always win
The bonds of trust grow weak and thin
At work or home if we just fight
We miss the chance to make things right

Next is Accommodating hearts
Who give up theirs to keep all parts
They say Its fine just have your way
And let their own needs fade away
Its kind and gentle full of grace
But too much leaves an empty place
If one gives all and none gives back
The love and peace begin to crack

Then Compromise the middle way
You give a bit and so will I
Its fair its fast a middle place
But rarely leaves a smiling face
For both give up and both still feel
A tiny ache they couldn't heal

But Collaboration shines the most
Though rarely used it is the gold
We sit we talk we truly try
To see the world through the others eyes
Not I must win or You must lose
But let's make better wiser moves

With open minds and patient hearts
Together we create new starts
But back again to where we fall
That stubborn cold invisible wall
We speak but don't hear we push we shove
And lose the thread of trust and love
Each side believes they're in the right
And so, begins the endless fight

So how do we break down that wall
Its not that high its not that tall
But breaking it takes heart and care
A little peace a breath of air
Listen first just for a while
With gentle ears and not with guile
Pause your mind your need to speak
Let the other share what they seek

You'd be surprised what you will hear
When you remove your inner fear
Acknowledge first before you fight
Say I see your side You may be right
Then softly share your honest view
And see how kindness pulls you through
When we listen, walls grow thin
And suddenly we both can win
The room feels warm the voices low
The seeds of peace begin to grow

So next time anger starts to rise
And harsh words shoot like arrows and lies
Take a breath and see the wall
And choose to let your silence fall
Break the wall with patient grace
Let empathy take conflicts place
For when we feel both seen and heard
We find the power in a word

And if we all just take the time
To speak with care to heal not rhyme
Then maybe walls will start to fall
And love will stand where once stood a wall

ESSENCE

Conflict fades when hearts listen.

BOOKS FROM THE SAME AUTHOR

INNOVATE WITH CHATGPT

Harnessing AI's Potential for Creative Solutions

1. Introduction to ChatGPT
2. Advance Concepts of ChatGPT
3. Applications of ChatGPT
4. ChatGPT in the Educational Sector
5. The Significance of Domain Knowledge
6. Crafting Effective Prompts
7. Integrating ChatGPT
8. Collaboration between Humans and AI
9. The Evolution of AI Conversations
10. Challenges and Limitations of AI
11. Creativity and its Blocks Bonus Chapter

Appendix – First Time User

EFFECTIVE MANAGEMENT SKILLS FOR TECHNICAL PROFESSIONALS

NOTES

www.ingramcontent.com/pod-product-compliance
Lightning Source LLC
Chambersburg PA
CBHW062143160726
48282CB00027B/924
9789334279139